Being More Accountable at Work

Gerard Assey

Being More Accountable at Work

By

Gerard Assey

Published by:

Gerard Assey

19/18, Palli Arasan Street

Anna Nagar East

Chennai - 600 102

ISBN: 978-93-92492-49-5

(Image courtesy Gerd Altmann from Pixabay.com-Thank You)

Table of Contents

Introduction

In a world where success often hinges on collaboration and shared responsibilities, the concept of accountability plays a pivotal role. It serves as a cornerstone for personal growth, professional development, and organizational success. Understanding and embracing accountability can transform not only how we work but also how we live our lives.

The Importance of Accountability in Personal and Professional Life: Accountability is more than just a buzzword; it is a fundamental principle that guides our actions and decisions. In our personal lives, being accountable means taking ownership of our choices, actions, and their consequences. It is about being reliable, trustworthy, and true to our word.

In the professional realm, accountability is equally crucial. It fosters a culture of responsibility and commitment within teams and organizations. When individuals hold themselves and others accountable, they are more likely to achieve their goals, meet deadlines, and deliver high-quality work.

Purpose and Structure of the Book: The purpose of this book is to provide you with a comprehensive understanding of accountability and its practical application in the workplace. Through a combination of theory, real-life examples, and actionable strategies, you will learn how to cultivate a culture of accountability in your business or workplace.

The book is structured to guide you through the different aspects of accountability, starting with the

basics and gradually building up to more advanced concepts. Each chapter will delve into a specific aspect of accountability, providing you with the knowledge and tools you need to enhance your accountability skills and transform your workplace.
By the end of this book, you will not only understand what accountability is and why it is important, but you will also be equipped with the strategies and techniques to implement accountability effectively in your personal and professional life.

Reflect: Reflect on a time when you faced a challenge or setback in your personal or professional life. How did you respond? Did you take ownership of the situation, or did you blame others? What could you have done differently to demonstrate greater accountability? Write down your reflections and discuss them with a trusted friend or colleague.

Example: Sarah, a project manager, was responsible for overseeing a critical project for her company. Despite her best efforts, the project fell behind schedule, leading to frustration among team members and stakeholders. Instead of blaming external factors, Sarah took ownership of the situation. She acknowledged the challenges, identified areas for improvement, and worked with her team to develop a plan to get the project back on track. By demonstrating accountability, Sarah was able to regain the trust of her team and successfully complete the project.

Action Plan: Identify one area in your personal or professional life where you could improve your accountability. Set a specific goal for yourself and create a plan of action to achieve it. Share your goal and action plan with a mentor, coach, or colleague who can provide you with guidance and support.

In conclusion, accountability is not just a virtue; it is a skill that can be learned and mastered. By embracing accountability in your personal and professional life, you can unlock your full potential and achieve greater success. This book will serve as your guide on this journey, providing you with the knowledge, tools, and inspiration you need to be more accountable at work and in life.

Understanding Accountability

Accountability is a fundamental concept that underpins success and growth, both personally and professionally. It is about taking ownership of our actions, decisions, and outcomes, and being answerable for them. In essence, accountability is the willingness to answer for the results of our behaviors and actions.

Definition of Accountability: Accountability can be defined as the obligation or willingness to accept responsibility for one's actions. It involves being answerable to oneself and others for the outcomes of those actions. Accountability is not just about taking the blame when things go wrong, but also about acknowledging one's role in the success of a task or project.

Key Principles of Accountability: There are several key principles that underlie the concept of accountability:

- ✓ Clarity: Accountability requires clear expectations and goals to be set. When individuals know what is expected of them, they are more likely to take ownership of their actions.
- ✓ Responsibility: Accountability involves taking responsibility for one's actions, decisions, and their outcomes. It is about recognizing the impact of one's actions on oneself and others.
- ✓ Transparency: Accountability requires transparency in communication and actions. It

involves being open and honest about one's intentions, actions, and outcomes.

- ✓ Consequences: Accountability involves accepting the consequences of one's actions, whether positive or negative. It requires individuals to be willing to face the outcomes of their decisions and behaviors.

Difference between Responsibility and Accountability: While responsibility and accountability are often used interchangeably, they are distinct concepts:

- ✓ Responsibility refers to the duties and obligations assigned to a person in a particular role or position. It is about fulfilling those duties to the best of one's ability.
- ✓ Accountability, on the other hand, goes a step further. It involves not just fulfilling one's duties, but also being answerable for the outcomes of those duties. Accountability requires individuals to take ownership of their actions and decisions, and to accept responsibility for the results.

Reflect: Think about a recent project or task you were involved in where accountability played a role. Consider how clarity, responsibility, transparency, and consequences were evident in that situation. Write down your thoughts and reflect on how you can apply these principles in future projects.

Example: John was part of a team working on a marketing campaign for a new product launch. He was responsible for creating the campaign's visual elements. Despite facing challenges with the project timeline, John ensured clear communication with his team about his progress. He took responsibility for meeting his deadlines and was transparent about any delays. When the campaign was launched successfully, John celebrated the team's success and accepted praise for his role in it.

Action Plan: Identify a task or project you are currently working on where you can apply the principles of accountability. Set clear goals and expectations for yourself, communicate openly with your team about your progress, and take ownership of the outcomes, whether positive or negative. Reflect on your experience and consider how you can further enhance your accountability in future projects.

Exercise: Create a personal accountability chart listing your current responsibilities and how you can take ownership of them.

Self-Reflection Question: How do you define accountability, and how does your definition influence your actions in the workplace?

Implementation Guide: Develop a personal accountability plan outlining specific actions you will take to enhance your accountability at work.

Why is Accountability Important in the Workplace? The Benefits

In the fast-paced and competitive world of business, accountability is not just a buzzword; it is a critical component of success. Accountability in the workplace refers to the responsibility of individuals to achieve their goals and fulfill their duties. It is about holding oneself and others answerable for their actions, decisions, and results.

Benefits of Accountability for Individuals, Teams, and Organizations: Accountability offers a wide range of benefits for individuals, teams, and organizations alike.

- ✓ For individuals, being accountable can lead to increased motivation, productivity, and job satisfaction. It can also help individuals develop valuable skills such as time management, problem-solving, and decision-making.
- ✓ For teams, accountability fosters a sense of unity and collaboration. When team members hold themselves and each other accountable, they are more likely to work together towards common goals and support one another in achieving them. This can lead to higher levels of team performance and success.
- ✓ For organizations, accountability is essential for achieving strategic objectives and maintaining a competitive edge. When employees are accountable for their actions, it can lead to improved financial performance,

better decision-making, and a stronger organizational culture.

Impact of Accountability on Performance, Trust, and Culture: Accountability has a profound impact on various aspects of workplace dynamics:

- ✓ Performance: Accountability drives performance by setting clear expectations and goals. When individuals know what is expected of them and are held accountable for their performance, they are more likely to strive for excellence.
- ✓ Trust: Accountability builds trust among team members and between employees and leaders. When individuals hold themselves accountable and follow through on their commitments, trust is strengthened, leading to better relationships and collaboration.
- ✓ Culture: Accountability contributes to a positive organizational culture. When accountability is valued and practiced at all levels of the organization, it creates a culture of responsibility, integrity, and transparency.

Case Studies or Examples Illustrating the Benefits of Accountability:

Case Study 1: Company X implemented a performance accountability system that required employees to set quarterly goals and report on their progress. As a result, employee engagement and productivity increased, leading to a 20% improvement in overall performance.

Case Study 2: Team Y adopted a culture of accountability where team members held each other accountable for meeting project deadlines and delivering high-quality work. This resulted in a more cohesive and efficient team, leading to a 30% reduction in project timelines.

Reflect: Reflect on a recent experience in your workplace where accountability played a role. Consider how accountability impacted the outcome of that experience and what could have been done differently to enhance accountability. Write down your reflections and discuss them with a colleague or mentor.

Action Plan: Identify one area in your work where you can improve accountability. Set a specific goal related to that area and create a plan of action to achieve it. Share your goal and action plan with a colleague or supervisor who can provide you with feedback and support.

Exercise: Conduct a team accountability assessment to evaluate the current level of accountability within your team.

Self-Reflection Question: What benefits do you personally experience when you are accountable in your work?

Implementation Guide: Create a team accountability action plan to improve accountability within your team, including setting goals and defining accountability measures.

Consequences of a Lack of Accountability at Work

In any organization, accountability is crucial for maintaining productivity, efficiency, and overall success. When accountability is lacking, the consequences can be significant, affecting not only individual performance but also team dynamics and organizational culture. In this chapter, we will explore the negative effects of a lack of accountability, common challenges faced in a workplace with low accountability, and real-life examples of companies or teams that have suffered due to this issue.

Negative Effects of a Lack of Accountability:

- ✓ Missed Deadlines: When individuals or teams are not held accountable for their work, deadlines are more likely to be missed, leading to delays in project completion and potential financial losses for the organization.
- ✓ Poor Quality of Work: Without accountability, there is less incentive for individuals to deliver high-quality work. This can result in subpar outcomes that do not meet the organization's standards or the needs of its customers.
- ✓ Low Morale: A lack of accountability can lead to frustration and low morale among team members. When individuals perceive that others are not pulling their weight or are not being held accountable for their actions, it can create resentment and a sense of unfairness.
- ✓ Decreased Trust: Accountability is essential for building trust among team members and between employees and leaders. When

accountability is lacking, trust erodes, leading to strained relationships and communication breakdowns.

- ✓ Increased Risk of Errors: Without accountability, there is a higher risk of errors and mistakes occurring in the workplace. This can have serious consequences, particularly in industries where accuracy and precision are critical.

Common Challenges Faced in a Workplace with Low Accountability:

- ✓ Blame-Shifting: In a low-accountability environment, individuals may be quick to shift blame onto others rather than take responsibility for their actions. This can create a culture of finger-pointing and defensiveness.
- ✓ Lack of Clarity: When expectations and responsibilities are not clearly defined, it can be challenging for individuals to know what is expected of them and how to prioritize their work.
- ✓ Poor Communication: Accountability is closely linked to communication. In a workplace with low accountability, communication breakdowns are common, leading to misunderstandings and inefficiencies.
- ✓ Resistance to Change: Without accountability, individuals may be resistant to change and hesitant to adopt new processes or ways of working.
- ✓ Negative Organizational Culture: A lack of accountability can contribute to a negative organizational culture characterized by low morale, distrust, and disengagement.

Real-Life Examples of Companies or Teams that Suffered Due to Lack of Accountability:

- ✓ Enron: The Enron scandal is a prominent example of a company that suffered due to a lack of accountability. Executives engaged in fraudulent accounting practices, leading to the company's bankruptcy and the loss of thousands of jobs.
- ✓ Volkswagen: Volkswagen faced a major crisis when it was revealed that the company had installed software in its vehicles to cheat emissions tests. This scandal was attributed in part to a lack of accountability within the company.
- ✓ Wells Fargo: Wells Fargo came under scrutiny for opening millions of unauthorized accounts on behalf of its customers. This scandal was attributed to a lack of accountability among employees and management.

Reflect: Think about a time when you experienced the negative effects of a lack of accountability in your workplace. Consider how these effects impacted you and those around you. Write down your thoughts and reflect on what could have been done differently to prevent or address these issues.

Example: Sarah worked for a company where accountability was lacking. Deadlines were frequently missed, and there was a culture of blame-shifting among team members. This led to a decline in morale and productivity. Sarah felt frustrated and de-motivated, as she was often left to pick up the slack for others' mistakes.

Action Plan: Identify one area in your workplace where accountability is lacking and brainstorm strategies to address it. This could involve setting clear expectations, implementing accountability mechanisms, or fostering a culture of openness and transparency. Share your ideas with a colleague or supervisor and work together to implement them.

Exercise: Role-play scenarios depicting the negative consequences of a lack of accountability and brainstorm solutions.

Self-Reflection Question: Have you ever experienced or witnessed the negative effects of a lack of accountability in the workplace?

Implementation Guide: Develop a personal accountability improvement plan to address any areas where you may be lacking in accountability.

Understanding the Stages of Accountability

Accountability is not a binary concept; rather, it exists along a continuum that reflects the progression of an individual's mindset and behavior. Understanding the stages of accountability can help individuals recognize where they are on this continuum and take steps to move toward greater accountability.

The Stages of Accountability:

- ✓ Denial: At the denial stage, individuals are unwilling or unable to acknowledge their role or responsibility in a situation. They may deny that a problem exists or that they played a part in creating it. For example, a team member might deny missing a deadline despite evidence to the contrary.
- ✓ Blame: In the blame stage, individuals acknowledge that a problem exists but attribute it to external factors or other people. They shift responsibility away from themselves and onto others. For example, a manager might blame a team member for a project failure instead of taking ownership of their role in overseeing the project.
- ✓ Responsibility: At the responsibility stage, individuals accept that they have a role in a situation and take ownership of their actions. They recognize that their choices and behaviors have contributed to the outcome, whether positive or negative. For example, a team member might take responsibility for a mistake they made and work to rectify it.

- ✓ Accountability: The highest stage of accountability, accountability involves not only taking responsibility for one's actions but also actively seeking to make amends and prevent future mistakes. Individuals at this stage are proactive in identifying areas for improvement and are committed to learning from their experiences. For example, a leader might hold themselves accountable for a team's failure by implementing new processes to ensure it does not happen again.

Self-Assessment Exercise: Consider a recent situation where something went wrong in your work or personal life. Reflect on your initial response to the situation. Did you deny that there was a problem? Did you blame others for the outcome? Or did you take responsibility for your role in the situation? Based on your reflection, identify which stage of accountability you were in at that time.

Example: Sarah, a project manager, was overseeing a team responsible for launching a new product. The launch was delayed due to a miscommunication between team members, resulting in frustration among stakeholders. Initially, Sarah was tempted to blame the team members involved for the delay, citing their lack of communication. However, after reflecting on the situation, she realized that as the project manager, she was ultimately responsible for ensuring clear communication among team members. She took ownership of the miscommunication and implemented new processes to prevent similar issues in the future, demonstrating accountability.

Action Plan: Identify a situation in your work or personal life where you are currently facing a challenge. Reflect on your initial response to the situation and consider whether you could approach it from a more accountable mindset. Set a goal for yourself to move toward greater accountability in this situation. This could involve acknowledging your role in the problem, taking proactive steps to address it, and learning from the experience to prevent similar issues in the future. Share your goal with a colleague or mentor who can support you in achieving it.

Exercise: Identify a recent situation where you moved through the stages of accountability and analyze your progression.

Self-Reflection Question: What stage of accountability do you find yourself in most often, and what steps can you take to progress to the next level?

Implementation Guide: Create a roadmap for moving through the stages of accountability, including specific actions for each stage.

Steps to Accountability in Your Business/ Workplace

Fostering accountability in the workplace is essential for achieving organizational goals and maintaining a high level of performance. It requires a concerted effort from both leaders and employees to create a culture where accountability is valued and practiced. In this chapter, we will explore practical steps to foster accountability in the workplace, how to create a culture of accountability, and tips for setting clear expectations and goals.

Practical Steps to Foster Accountability in the Workplace:

- ✓ Lead by Example: Leaders play a crucial role in setting the tone for accountability in the workplace. They should model accountable behavior by taking ownership of their actions, admitting mistakes, and following through on commitments.
- ✓ Set Clear Expectations: Clearly define roles, responsibilities, and expectations for each team member. Ensure that everyone understands what is expected of them and how their performance will be evaluated.
- ✓ Establish Goals and Key Performance Indicators (KPIs): Set SMART (Specific, Measurable, Achievable, Relevant, Time-bound) goals for individuals and teams. Define KPIs that align with organizational objectives and track progress regularly.
- ✓ Provide Feedback and Coaching: Regularly provide constructive feedback to employees

on their performance. Offer coaching and support to help them improve and meet their goals.

- ✓ Implement Accountability Mechanisms: Establish accountability mechanisms such as regular check-ins, performance reviews, and peer evaluations to monitor progress and ensure accountability.

Creating a Culture of Accountability:

- ✓ Communicate Openly: Foster a culture of open communication where employees feel comfortable discussing challenges, asking for help, and providing feedback.
- ✓ Encourage Ownership: Encourage employees to take ownership of their work and decisions. Empower them to find solutions to problems and make decisions within their scope of authority.
- ✓ Recognize and Reward Accountability: Recognize and reward employees who demonstrate accountability in their work. This can help reinforce accountable behavior and motivate others to follow suit.
- ✓ Address Non-Accountable Behavior: Address non-accountable behavior promptly and constructively. Provide feedback and guidance on how to improve, and set clear expectations for future behavior.

Tips for Setting Clear Expectations and Goals:

- ✓ Be Specific: Clearly define what needs to be achieved and by when. Avoid vague or ambiguous goals that can lead to confusion.

- ✓ Make Goals Measurable: Ensure that goals are measurable so that progress can be tracked and evaluated objectively.
- ✓ Align Goals with Organizational Objectives: Ensure that individual and team goals are aligned with the broader objectives of the organization. This helps to create a sense of purpose and direction.
- ✓ Provide Support and Resources: Ensure that employees have the necessary support, resources, and training to achieve their goals. Address any barriers or challenges that may hinder their progress.

Example: Sarah, a team leader, wanted to foster greater accountability within her team. She started by setting clear expectations and goals for each team member, ensuring that they understood what was expected of them. She also implemented regular check-ins to monitor progress and provide feedback. By leading by example and creating a culture of accountability, Sarah was able to improve team performance and morale.

Action Plan: Identify one area in your workplace where accountability could be improved. Set a specific goal for improving accountability in that area and create a plan of action to achieve it. Share your goal with your team or supervisor and seek their support in implementing your plan. Regularly review your progress and adjust your approach as needed to achieve your goal.
Exercise: Conduct a SWOT analysis (Strengths, Weaknesses, Opportunities, Threats) of your current accountability practices.

Self-Reflection Question: What steps can you take to foster a culture of accountability in your workplace?
Implementation Guide: Develop an accountability implementation plan for your organization, including timelines and responsible parties.

Understanding the Accountability Ladder

The accountability ladder is a powerful model that illustrates the different stages of accountability that individuals can exhibit in the workplace. By understanding this model, individuals can identify where they currently stand on the ladder and take steps to climb to higher levels of accountability. In this chapter, we will explore the accountability ladder model, how to climb the ladder from bottom rungs (laying blame) to top rungs (taking ownership), and provide examples of behaviors at each rung of the ladder.

Explanation of the Accountability Ladder Model: The accountability ladder consists of eight rungs, each representing a different level of accountability. The ladder is divided into two sections: the lower rungs, which represent a lack of accountability, and the higher rungs, which represent increasing levels of accountability.

- ✓ Lay Blame: At the bottom of the ladder is the rung where individuals lay blame for problems or failures on external factors or other people. They refuse to take responsibility for their actions and often point fingers at others.
- ✓ Justify: The next rung is where individuals justify their actions or decisions, often by providing excuses or rationalizations. They may acknowledge that a problem exists but believe they had valid reasons for their behavior.

- ✓ Shame: On this rung, individuals feel ashamed or guilty about their actions but may not take any concrete steps to address the situation. They may dwell on their mistakes without taking proactive measures to correct them.
- ✓ Obligation: At this rung, individuals feel obligated to take action but may do so reluctantly or without a genuine commitment. They may fulfill their responsibilities out of a sense of duty rather than a desire to make a positive impact.
- ✓ Responsibility: This rung represents a significant shift in mindset, where individuals take ownership of their actions and their consequences. They recognize their role in a situation and are willing to do what it takes to address it.
- ✓ Self-Motivated: On this rung, individuals are not only willing to take responsibility but are also motivated to take action. They actively seek out opportunities to improve and make a positive impact.
- ✓ Seek Solutions: At this rung, individuals not only take responsibility for their actions but also actively seek solutions to problems. They are proactive in identifying and addressing issues before they escalate.
- ✓ Make It Right: The top rung of the ladder is where individuals not only seek solutions but also take decisive action to make things right. They go above and beyond to rectify the situation and ensure that similar issues do not occur in the future.

How to Climb the Ladder from Bottom Rungs to Top Rungs: Climbing the accountability ladder requires a conscious effort to change behaviors and mindset. Here are some steps to help you climb the ladder:

- ✓ Self-Reflection: Reflect on your current behavior and identify which rung of the ladder you are on. Be honest with yourself about where you can improve.
- ✓ Take Ownership: Accept responsibility for your actions and their consequences. Avoid blaming others or making excuses.
- ✓ Seek Feedback: Ask for feedback from colleagues, supervisors, or mentors on how you can improve your accountability.
- ✓ Set Goals: Set specific, achievable goals for yourself to climb the ladder. Break down larger goals into smaller, manageable steps.
- ✓ Practice Accountability: Practice holding yourself accountable in everyday situations. Look for opportunities to take ownership and seek solutions.

Examples of Behaviors at Each Rung of the Ladder:

- ✓ Lay Blame: "It's not my fault that the project failed. The client kept changing the requirements."
- ✓ Justify: "I had to leave work early because traffic was terrible. It's not like I could control that."
- ✓ Shame: "I feel really bad about missing the deadline, but there was nothing I could do about it."

- ✓ Obligation: "I guess I have to stay late to finish this report, even though I don't really want to."
- ✓ Responsibility: "I realize that I made a mistake in the presentation, and I'm committed to doing better next time."
- ✓ Self-Motivated: "I want to improve my communication skills, so I'm going to enroll in a course to learn how to be more effective."
- ✓ Seek Solutions: "I see that there's a problem with our current process, so I'm going to research and propose a more efficient solution."
- ✓ Make It Right: "I take full responsibility for the error in the report, and I'm going to work overtime to fix it and ensure it doesn't happen again."

Reflect: Reflect on a recent situation where you may have exhibited behavior from the lower rungs of the ladder (laying blame, justifying, etc.). Consider how you could have approached the situation differently to exhibit behavior from the higher rungs (taking ownership, seeking solutions, etc.). Write down your thoughts and discuss them with a colleague or mentor to gain their perspective.

Action Plan: Choose one specific behavior from the accountability ladder that you would like to improve (e.g., taking more ownership, seeking solutions). Set a goal for yourself to exhibit that behavior in a specific situation within the next week. Keep a journal of your progress and reflect on how your actions impact your accountability. Share your progress with a colleague or supervisor for feedback and support.

Exercise: Role-play scenarios illustrating different rungs of the accountability ladder and discuss how each rung impacts outcomes.
Self-Reflection Question: Which rung of the accountability ladder do you most often find yourself on, and what actions can you take to climb higher?
Implementation Guide: Create a personal accountability ladder plan, setting goals for climbing the ladder and overcoming obstacles.

How to Use the Accountability Ladder in Leadership

Leaders play a crucial role in promoting accountability within their teams and organizations. By understanding and utilizing the accountability ladder model, leaders can effectively guide their team members to take ownership of their actions, decisions, and outcomes. In this chapter, we will explore the role of leaders in promoting accountability, strategies for leaders to model accountability, and how leaders can coach their team members to climb the accountability ladder.

Role of Leaders in Promoting Accountability: Leaders serve as role models for their teams, and their behavior sets the tone for the entire organization. In promoting accountability, leaders should:

- ✓ Set Clear Expectations: Clearly communicate expectations for performance, behavior, and outcomes to team members. Ensure that goals are specific, measurable, achievable, relevant, and time-bound (SMART).
- ✓ Provide Support and Resources: Ensure that team members have the necessary support, resources, and training to meet their goals. Address any barriers or challenges that may hinder their progress.
- ✓ Encourage Open Communication: Foster a culture of open communication where team members feel comfortable discussing challenges, asking for help, and providing feedback.

- ✓ Recognize and Reward Accountability: Acknowledge and reward team members who demonstrate accountability in their work. This can help reinforce accountable behavior and motivate others to follow suit.

Strategies for Leaders to Model Accountability:

- ✓ Take Ownership: Leaders should lead by example and take ownership of their actions, decisions, and outcomes. They should avoid blaming others or making excuses.
- ✓ Admit Mistakes: Leaders should be willing to admit when they make mistakes and take steps to rectify them. This demonstrates humility and a commitment to learning and improvement.
- ✓ Follow Through on Commitments: Leaders should follow through on their commitments and promises. This builds trust with team members and sets a positive example for accountability.
- ✓ Seek Feedback: Leaders should actively seek feedback from team members, peers, and supervisors on how they can improve their accountability and leadership effectiveness.

How Leaders Can Coach Their Team Members to Climb the Accountability Ladder:

- ✓ Provide Constructive Feedback: Regularly provide feedback to team members on their performance and behavior. Be specific about areas where they can improve and offer guidance on how to do so.
- ✓ Set Development Goals: Work with team members to set development goals that align

with their career aspirations and the organization's objectives. Provide support and resources to help them achieve these goals.

- ✓ Encourage Self-Reflection: Encourage team members to reflect on their actions and behaviors and identify areas where they can improve their accountability. Offer guidance on how to approach situations differently in the future.
- ✓ Celebrate Progress: Acknowledge and celebrate the progress that team members make in improving their accountability. This can help motivate them to continue climbing the accountability ladder.

Example: John, a team leader, noticed that one of his team members, Sarah, was struggling to meet deadlines and take ownership of her work. Instead of reprimanding her, John took a coaching approach. He had a candid conversation with Sarah about her challenges and helped her identify specific actions she could take to improve her accountability. He provided ongoing support and encouragement, and Sarah was able to climb the accountability ladder and become a more effective team member.

Action Plan: Identify one area in your leadership role where you can improve your accountability. Set a specific goal for yourself to model accountability in that area and create a plan of action to achieve it. Share your goal with a mentor or colleague who can provide you with feedback and support. Regularly assess your progress and adjust your approach as needed to achieve your goal.

Exercise: Practice coaching a team member to climb the accountability ladder using the ladder model.
Self-Reflection Question: How can you model accountable behavior as a leader to inspire your team?
Implementation Guide: Develop a leadership accountability plan, including strategies for modeling accountability and coaching team members.

Accountability in Decision-Making

In any organization, decision-making is a critical process that can greatly impact its success. Accountability in decision-making ensures that individuals are responsible for the choices they make and the outcomes of those choices. This chapter explores the importance of accountability in decision-making and how it enhances the quality and effectiveness of decisions.

Key Concepts:
Accountability in decision-making refers to the responsibility individuals or groups have for the decisions they make and the consequences of those decisions. It involves transparency, honesty, and taking ownership of one's actions. Individual accountability focuses on the responsibility of individuals for their decisions, while collective accountability involves the responsibility of groups or teams for decisions made collectively. Transparency and clarity in decision-making processes are essential for accountability, as they ensure that decisions are made based on relevant information and are understood by all stakeholders.

Strategies for Accountability in Decision-Making:
Establishing Clear Decision-Making Processes:

- ✓ Action Plan: Define clear processes for making decisions, including roles, responsibilities, and decision criteria.
- ✓ Example: A team creates a decision matrix to outline how decisions will be made, ensuring

everyone understands their role in the process.

Ensuring Open Communication:

- ✓ Action Plan: Encourage open dialogue and feedback during the decision-making process.
- ✓ Example: A leader holds regular meetings to discuss decisions openly and invites team members to provide input.

Documenting Decisions:

- ✓ Action Plan: Document decisions, including rationale and outcomes, to ensure accountability.
- ✓ Example: A team keeps a decision log to track the decisions made, the reasons behind them, and the results.

Reviewing and Evaluating Decisions:

- ✓ Action Plan: Establish a process for reviewing and evaluating decisions to learn from successes and failures.
- ✓ Example: An organization conducts post-mortem reviews after major decisions to assess their impact and identify areas for improvement.

Holding Individuals Accountable:

- ✓ Action Plan: Clearly define roles and responsibilities for decision-making and hold individuals accountable for their decisions.
- ✓ Example: A manager holds regular performance reviews with team members to discuss their decision-making effectiveness.

Benefits of Accountability in Decision-Making:

Accountability in decision-making leads to improved quality of decisions, as individuals are more likely to carefully consider their choices and their potential impact. It also increases trust and transparency within the organization, as stakeholders can see that decisions are made fairly and responsibly. Additionally, accountability fosters collaboration and teamwork, as individuals are more willing to work together when they know they will be held accountable for the outcomes.

In conclusion, accountability in decision-making is essential for organizational success. By implementing strategies for accountability, leaders can ensure that decisions are made thoughtfully and responsibly, leading to better outcomes for the organization as a whole. It is crucial for leaders to foster a culture of accountability within their organizations and to lead by example in their own decision-making processes.

Signs of a Workplace with Great Accountability

A workplace with a strong culture of accountability is characterized by a sense of responsibility, ownership, and commitment among its employees. In such environments, individuals and teams are empowered to take ownership of their actions and outcomes, leading to higher levels of performance and success. In this chapter, we will explore the signs of a workplace with great accountability, the characteristics of accountable individuals and teams, and showcase case studies of organizations known for their strong culture of accountability.

Indicators of a High-Accountability Workplace:

- ✓ Clear Communication: In a high-accountability workplace, communication is open, honest, and transparent. Expectations, goals, and feedback are clearly communicated to all employees.
- ✓ Ownership of Results: Employees in a high-accountability workplace take ownership of their actions and outcomes. They do not blame others for failures but instead focus on finding solutions and learning from mistakes.
- ✓ Proactive Problem-Solving: Individuals and teams in a high-accountability workplace are proactive in identifying and addressing problems. They take initiative to find solutions rather than waiting for others to take action.
- ✓ Trust and Respect: There is a high level of trust and respect among employees in a high-accountability workplace. Team members trust

each other to fulfill their responsibilities and hold themselves accountable.

- ✓ Continuous Improvement: A culture of accountability fosters a commitment to continuous improvement. Employees are always looking for ways to enhance their performance and achieve better results.

Characteristics of Accountable Individuals and Teams:

- ✓ Responsibility: Accountable individuals take responsibility for their actions and outcomes. They do not make excuses or blame others for failures.
- ✓ Integrity: Accountable individuals demonstrate integrity in their actions and decisions. They adhere to ethical standards and do what is right, even when it is difficult.
- ✓ Communication: Accountable individuals communicate openly and honestly with others. They are transparent about their intentions, actions, and outcomes.
- ✓ Adaptability: Accountable individuals are adaptable and able to respond effectively to change. They are willing to adjust their approach in response to new information or circumstances.
- ✓ Collaboration: Accountable individuals work collaboratively with others to achieve common goals. They recognize the importance of teamwork and support their colleagues in achieving success.

Case Studies Showcasing Organizations Known for Their Strong Culture of Accountability:

- ✓ Google: Google is known for its strong culture of accountability, which is reflected in its emphasis on transparency, collaboration, and innovation. Employees are empowered to take ownership of their projects and are held accountable for their outcomes.
- ✓ Southwest Airlines: Southwest Airlines is another example of an organization with a strong culture of accountability. The company's success is attributed in part to its focus on accountability at all levels, from top executives to front-line employees.
- ✓ Zappos: Zappos, an online shoe and clothing retailer, is known for its commitment to accountability and customer service. Employees are encouraged to take ownership of customer interactions and are empowered to make decisions to ensure customer satisfaction.

Reflect: Reflect on your current workplace environment and identify areas where accountability could be improved. Consider how implementing the characteristics of a high-accountability workplace could benefit your organization. Write down your thoughts and discuss them with a colleague or supervisor.

Example: Sarah works for a company that has a strong culture of accountability. She and her team are empowered to take ownership of their projects and are held accountable for their outcomes. As a result, Sarah feels more motivated and engaged in her work, and the team consistently achieves high levels of performance.

Action Plan: Identify one area in your work where you can demonstrate greater accountability. Set a specific goal for yourself to improve accountability in that area and create a plan of action to achieve it. Share your goal with a colleague or mentor who can provide you with feedback and support. Regularly assess your progress and adjust your approach as needed to achieve your goal.

Exercise: Conduct a workplace accountability survey to assess the current level of accountability in your organization.

Self-Reflection Question: What signs of accountability do you observe in your workplace, and how can they be further promoted?

Implementation Guide: Create a workplace accountability improvement plan based on survey results, including action items and timelines.

Demonstrating Accountability at Work

Demonstrating accountability in the workplace is essential for building trust, fostering teamwork, and achieving success. It involves taking ownership of one's actions, decisions, and outcomes, and being transparent and honest in all professional interactions. In this chapter, we will explore practical examples of demonstrating accountability in various scenarios, as well as role-playing exercises for readers to practice accountability in different situations.

Practical Examples of Demonstrating Accountability:

- ✓ Admitting Mistakes: When you make a mistake, admit it openly and take responsibility for the consequences. For example, if you miss a deadline, acknowledge the error and work with your team to find a solution.
- ✓ Meeting Deadlines: Honor your commitments by meeting deadlines and delivering work on time. If you anticipate that you may not be able to meet a deadline, communicate proactively and propose a new timeline.
- ✓ Seeking Feedback: Actively seek feedback from colleagues, supervisors, and clients on your work. Use this feedback to identify areas for improvement and take action to address them.
- ✓ Following Through on Commitments: When you make a commitment to a colleague or

supervisor, follow through on it. This demonstrates reliability and trustworthiness.

- ✓ Taking Initiative: Look for opportunities to take on new challenges and projects. Taking initiative shows that you are proactive and committed to the success of the organization.

Role-Playing Exercises:

- ✓ Admitting Mistakes: In pairs, role-play a scenario where one person makes a mistake and must admit it to their supervisor or team. Practice being honest and taking responsibility for the mistake, and discuss how you could have handled the situation differently.
- ✓ Meeting Deadlines: In pairs, role-play a scenario where one person is struggling to meet a deadline. Practice communicating proactively with your team and proposing a new timeline. Discuss strategies for better time management and prioritization.
- ✓ Seeking Feedback: In pairs, role-play a scenario where one person is seeking feedback from a colleague on their work. Practice asking for specific feedback and receiving it gracefully. Discuss how you can use the feedback to improve your performance.
- ✓ Following Through on Commitments: In pairs, role-play a scenario where one person has failed to follow through on a commitment. Practice acknowledging the oversight and proposing a solution. Discuss how you can prevent similar situations in the future.
- ✓ Taking Initiative: In pairs, role-play a scenario where one person is taking initiative on a new

project. Practice communicating your ideas clearly and persuasively. Discuss how you can continue to take initiative in your role.

Example: Sarah was working on a project with a tight deadline. Despite her best efforts, she realized that she would not be able to meet the deadline due to unforeseen circumstances. Instead of hiding the issue or blaming others, Sarah immediately informed her team and proposed a revised timeline. She took responsibility for the delay and worked with her team to ensure that the project was completed successfully, demonstrating accountability in action.

Action Plan: Choose one of the practical examples of demonstrating accountability mentioned above that you would like to focus on improving. Set a specific goal for yourself to demonstrate accountability in that area and create a plan of action to achieve it. Practice the role-playing exercises with a colleague or mentor to refine your skills. Regularly assess your progress and adjust your approach as needed to achieve your goal.

Exercise: Write a scenario where you demonstrate accountability in a challenging situation and discuss it with a peer for feedback.

Self-Reflection Question: How do you typically respond to mistakes or setbacks at work, and how can you improve your accountability in these situations?

Implementation Guide: Develop a personal accountability action plan for demonstrating accountability in various work scenarios.

How to Encourage, Promote and Increase Accountability

Encouraging and promoting accountability in the workplace is crucial for fostering a culture of trust, transparency, and high performance. Leaders play a key role in creating an environment where accountability thrives, and it is essential to integrate accountability into the organization's culture and performance management systems. In this chapter, we will explore strategies for leaders to encourage accountability, ways to build accountability into performance management systems, and how to create a supportive environment for accountability to flourish.

Strategies for Leaders to Encourage Accountability:

- ✓ Lead by Example: Leaders should model accountable behavior by taking ownership of their actions and decisions. They should demonstrate transparency, honesty, and a willingness to admit mistakes.
- ✓ Set Clear Expectations: Clearly communicate expectations for performance, behavior, and outcomes to employees. Ensure that goals are specific, measurable, achievable, relevant, and time-bound (SMART).
- ✓ Provide Support and Resources: Ensure that employees have the necessary support, resources, and training to meet their goals. Address any barriers or challenges that may hinder their progress.

- ✓ Foster Open Communication: Encourage open and honest communication among team members. Create a safe space for employees to voice their concerns, ask for help, and provide feedback.
- ✓ Recognize and Reward Accountability: Acknowledge and reward employees who demonstrate accountability in their work. This can be done through public recognition, bonuses, or other incentives.

Building Accountability into Performance Management Systems:

- ✓ Set Clear Goals and Objectives: Establish clear, measurable goals and objectives for employees that align with the organization's strategic objectives.
- ✓ Regular Performance Reviews: Conduct regular performance reviews to assess progress towards goals and provide feedback on areas for improvement.
- ✓ Accountability Metrics: Include accountability metrics in performance evaluations to measure how well employees are taking ownership of their work and outcomes.
- ✓ Development Plans: Create individual development plans that outline specific actions employees can take to improve their accountability and performance.

Creating a Supportive Environment for Accountability to Thrive:

- ✓ Establish Trust: Build trust among team members by demonstrating integrity, fairness, and consistency in your actions.

- ✓ Encourage Collaboration: Foster a collaborative work environment where team members support each other and work together towards common goals.
- ✓ Provide Feedback and Coaching: Offer regular feedback and coaching to employees to help them improve their accountability and performance.
- ✓ Celebrate Successes: Celebrate achievements and milestones as a team to reinforce a culture of accountability and recognition.

Example: John, a manager, wanted to promote accountability within his team. He started by setting clear expectations for performance and behavior and providing ongoing support and feedback to his team members. He also implemented a performance management system that included regular performance reviews and accountability metrics. As a result, John's team became more engaged and motivated, leading to improved performance and outcomes.

Action Plan: Identify one area in your organization where accountability could be improved. Set a specific goal for yourself to promote accountability in that area and create a plan of action to achieve it. Share your goal with your team or supervisor and seek their support in implementing your plan. Regularly review your progress and adjust your approach as needed to achieve your goal.
Exercise: Brainstorm with your team ways to promote accountability in your workplace and create a shared accountability action plan.

Self-Reflection Question: How can you as a leader foster a culture of accountability within your team or organization?
Implementation Guide: Develop a leadership accountability development plan, including strategies for promoting accountability among team members and tracking progress.

Strategies and Action Plans to Build in a Sense of Accountability in Employees

Building a sense of accountability among employees is crucial for the success of any organization. Here are various strategies with detailed action plans and examples that leaders and organizations can adopt:

Set Clear Expectations:

- ✓ Action Plan: Clearly define roles, responsibilities, and expectations for each employee.
- ✓ Example: A manager sets specific and measurable goals for their team members and regularly communicates expectations to ensure clarity.

Provide Regular Feedback:

- ✓ Action Plan: Schedule regular feedback sessions to discuss performance and progress.
- ✓ Example: A supervisor meets with employees quarterly to review their goals and provide constructive feedback on their performance.

Encourage Ownership:

- ✓ Action Plan: Empower employees to make decisions and take ownership of their work.
- ✓ Example: A leader allows team members to take the lead on projects and supports them in making decisions.

Reward Accountability:

- ✓ Action Plan: Recognize and reward employees who demonstrate accountability in their work.

- ✓ Example: An organization implements an employee recognition program that rewards individuals for taking ownership and achieving results.

Lead by Example:

- ✓ Action Plan: Demonstrate accountable behavior in your own actions and decisions.
- ✓ Example: A manager admits when they make a mistake and takes responsibility for finding a solution.

Provide Training and Development:

- ✓ Action Plan: Offer training programs to help employees develop accountability skills.
- ✓ Example: An organization provides workshops on time management and goal setting to help employees take ownership of their work.

Create a Supportive Environment:

- ✓ Action Plan: Foster a culture of trust and collaboration where employees feel supported.
- ✓ Example: A team holds regular meetings to discuss challenges openly and brainstorm solutions together.

Establish Consequences for Non-Accountability:

- ✓ Action Plan: Clearly communicate the consequences of not meeting expectations.
- ✓ Example: An organization implements a performance improvement plan for employees who consistently fail to meet their goals.

Provide Resources and Tools:

- ✓ Action Plan: Ensure employees have the necessary resources and tools to succeed.
- ✓ Example: An organization invests in project management software to help employees track their progress and stay organized.

Celebrate Successes:

- ✓ Action Plan: Acknowledge and celebrate achievements, both big and small.
- ✓ Example: A team celebrates reaching a milestone on a project and recognizes the efforts of each team member.

By implementing these strategies and action plans, leaders and organizations can build a strong sense of accountability among employees, leading to increased productivity, improved performance, and a positive work culture.

Setting Accountability Goals

Setting accountability goals is a powerful way to take ownership of your actions and outcomes. Here is a template you can use to set accountability goals:

Define the Goal:

- ✓ Clearly state the goal you want to achieve. Make sure it is specific, measurable, achievable, relevant, and time-bound (SMART).

Identify Accountability Measures:

- ✓ Determine how you will measure progress towards your goal. This could include specific metrics, milestones, or deadlines.

Set Action Steps:

- ✓ Outline the steps you need to take to achieve your goal. Break down larger goals into smaller, manageable tasks.

Establish a Timeline:

- ✓ Set a timeline for when you will complete each action step and achieve your goal. Be realistic but also challenge yourself to stay on track.

Plan for Challenges:

- ✓ Anticipate potential obstacles or challenges that may arise and develop strategies to overcome them.

Monitor Progress:

- ✓ Regularly review your progress towards your goal. Adjust your plan as needed to stay on track.

Celebrate Achievements:

- ✓ Celebrate your achievements, no matter how small. This will help you stay motivated and committed to your goal.

Example:

Goal: Improve time management skills to meet project deadlines more effectively.

Accountability Measures:

- ✓ Track the time spent on each task using a time tracking tool.
- ✓ Set weekly progress meetings with the team to review project timelines.

Action Steps:

- ✓ Identify time-wasting activities and eliminate or minimize them.
- ✓ Prioritize tasks based on urgency and importance.
- ✓ Use a calendar or task management tool to schedule and track deadlines.
- ✓ Delegate tasks when appropriate to free up time for high-priority tasks.

Timeline:

- ✓ By the end of the month, reduce time spent on non-essential tasks by 20%.
- ✓ Complete a time management course within the next three months.

Challenges:

- ✓ Distractions in the workplace.
- ✓ Balancing multiple projects and deadlines.

Action Plan:

- ✓ Identify specific time-wasting activities (e.g., excessive social media use) and set limits or restrictions to minimize them.
- ✓ Prioritize tasks using the Eisenhower Matrix and focus on high-priority tasks first.
- ✓ Use a calendar or task management tool to schedule deadlines and set reminders.

- ✓ Delegate tasks that can be handled by others to free up time for important tasks.

By following this template and creating a detailed action plan, you can set accountability goals that are achievable and impactful. Remember to review your progress regularly and adjust your plan as needed to stay on track.

Self-Assessment Tools for Ongoing Accountability Development

Self-assessment tools are valuable resources for ongoing accountability development. They allow individuals to reflect on their behaviors, actions, and attitudes related to accountability and identify areas for improvement. Here is a template for a self-assessment tool for accountability development:

Accountability Self-Assessment:

A. Responsibility

- ✓ I take ownership of my actions and decisions.
- ✓ I do not blame others for my mistakes.
- ✓ I follow through on commitments and promises.

B. Communication

- ✓ I communicate openly and honestly with others.
- ✓ I seek feedback from colleagues and supervisors.
- ✓ I express my expectations and needs clearly.

C. Problem-Solving

- ✓ I am proactive in identifying and addressing problems.
- ✓ I look for solutions rather than dwelling on problems.
- ✓ I take initiative to improve processes and outcomes.

D. Adaptability

- ✓ I am flexible and open to change.
- ✓ I adjust my approach based on feedback and new information.
- ✓ I embrace new challenges and opportunities for growth.

E. Collaboration

- ✓ I work well with others towards common goals.
- ✓ I support my colleagues and contribute to team success.
- ✓ I share knowledge and resources to help others succeed.

Action Plan:

- ✓ Review the self-assessment and identify areas where you scored lower or feel you need to improve.
- ✓ Set specific, measurable goals for improvement in those areas.
- ✓ Develop a plan of action with concrete steps you will take to achieve your goals.
- ✓ Implement your action plan and track your progress regularly.
- ✓ Reflect on your progress and adjust your goals and action plan as needed.

Example: Self-Assessment Score: A. Responsibility: 3/5 B. Communication: 4/5 C. Problem-Solving: 2/5 D. Adaptability: 3/5 E. Collaboration: 4/5

Action Plan:

- ✓ Responsibility: Focus on taking more ownership of my actions and decisions. Start by admitting mistakes openly and working on follow-through.
- ✓ Problem-Solving: Develop a proactive approach to problem-solving by identifying potential issues early and proposing solutions. Seek feedback from colleagues on my problem-solving skills.

- ✓ Adaptability: Embrace change more readily by seeking out new challenges and being open to feedback. Take on new responsibilities that stretch my skills and abilities.
- ✓ Collaboration: Continue to work well with others and actively seek out opportunities to collaborate on projects. Offer support and assistance to colleagues whenever possible.

By using this self-assessment tool and developing an action plan, individuals can take proactive steps to improve their accountability skills and contribute to a more productive and successful work environment.

Conclusion

In this book, we have explored the concept of accountability and its importance in the workplace. We have discussed the benefits of accountability, the consequences of its absence, and practical steps individuals and leaders can take to foster a culture of accountability.

Key Points Covered:

- ✓ Accountability is the act of taking ownership of one's actions, decisions, and outcomes.
- ✓ A high level of accountability leads to increased trust, improved performance, and a positive work culture.
- ✓ Leaders play a crucial role in promoting accountability by setting clear expectations, providing support, and modeling accountable behavior.
- ✓ Individuals can demonstrate accountability by admitting mistakes, meeting deadlines, seeking feedback, and taking initiative.

Importance of Accountability: Accountability is essential for personal and professional growth. It allows individuals to learn from their mistakes, improve their performance, and build trust with colleagues and supervisors. In a workplace with a strong culture of accountability, teams are more likely to achieve their goals and succeed in their endeavors.

Call to Action: As you reflect on the concepts and strategies discussed in this book, I encourage you to apply them to your own work and life. Identify areas where you can improve your accountability and set specific goals to do so. Remember that accountability is a journey, and it requires continuous effort and commitment. By taking ownership of your actions and decisions, you can make a positive impact on your work, your team, and your organization.

Final Thoughts: Accountability is not just a buzzword; it is a fundamental aspect of personal and professional success. By embracing accountability, you can unlock your full potential and achieve greatness in all areas of your life. I hope this book has inspired you to take the necessary steps to become more accountable and make a difference in your workplace and beyond.

Thank you for reading, and best of luck on your journey to greater accountability!

About the Author
'GERARD ASSEY'

Gerard Assey is a Graduate in Economics, a PGD in Management (HRD) and holds a Doctorate in Leadership. Gerard holds several International Qualifications in Sales, Debt Collection, Training & Teaching, and is a 'Fellow' of the prestigious 'Institute of Sales & Marketing Management'-UK, a Certified NLP Practitioner, a 'Certified Trainer', an 'Accredited Management Teacher-Behavioral Sciences', a 'Certified Competency Facilitator', a 'Certified Management Consultant'- (the International credentials of a professional management consultant, awarded in accordance with global standards of the ICMCI); and a Certification from the University of Michigan in 'Successful Negotiation: Essential Strategies and Skills'

He is also a Member of the 'National Association of Sales Professionals' backed with several years experience in varied industries, both in India and Overseas. He also holds an 'Etiquette Consultant' Certification from the USA (by Sue Fox, Author of Best Seller: 'Business Etiquette for Dummies'. She has trained some of the top celebrities' world over). He was also a recipient of a scholarship for extensive training in Japan on 'Corporate Management for India'.

Gerard Assey is 'Founder & Chief Corporate Trainer' of the Group: '**Citius, Altius, Fortius Unlimited**'- an organization that **celebrated 20 years of Glorious Service** in 2021, focusing on 3 Core Competencies:

People. Performance. Profit; in functional areas of Sales & Marketing, HR & Organizational Development, covering Recruitment, Training & Consultancy!

Having managed organizations with large Sales Forces in India & Overseas, his specialization cover extensive areas of Sales Training (All levels - Presentation, Negotiation, Key/ Strategic Accounts Management & Managerial Skills for all sectors), Bid Proposal/ Capture Planning/ Management Trainings, Retail Sales, Customer Service & Customer Retention Programs, Training for Prevention & Collection of Debt, Self & Personal Development Programs (Time Management, Teamwork & Team Building, Business Etiquette & Personal Grooming, Leadership & Managerial Skills, People Management Skills, Train-the-Trainer etc), including preparation of Custom-designed Business Manuals for Internal (HR, Induction, and Sales etc) & External use (Instruction, User Manuals).

Gerard has successfully conducted over 6060 Trainings & Workshops (as of Feb '24) all across India, Middle East, Africa, Europe & S.E. Asia. Besides public programs conducted regularly, both in India & Overseas, he has some of the top names as clients whom he services from Single Owners to large Public & Government undertakings, covering all sectors, for their in-house needs.

His website: www.CollectionSkills.com is the only one in this part of the world to be featured in the 'Collections & Credit Risk Magazine-USA' under 'Who's Who in Training' and ranks TOP, along with other websites listed below on most search engines.

Gerard is author of 109 books already (Feb 2024)

A few of our business related books:

1. Bite-sized Bits on Commonsense Management
2. Heart to Heart on Life's Principles'
3. How to become a Successful Manager
4. The Sales Professionals' Master Workbook of S.Y.S.T.E.M.S
5. The Professional Business Email Etiquette Handbook & Guide
6. The Professional Business Video-Conferencing Etiquette Handbook & Guide
7. Professional Presentation Skills
8. Exceptional Customer Service
9. Professional Tele-Marketing Skills
10. Professional Debt Collection Skills
11. The G.R.E.A.T. Sales & Service Workbook
12. Sales Training Advantage for Results (*The Ultimate Sales Training Manual to enable you stand out as a S.T.A.R.*)
13. CEO Daily Planner & Organizer
14. The Sales Professionals' Master Daily Planner
15. The Professional Debt Collector's Master Daily Planner
16. My Daily Planner & Organizer
17. MY EMERGENCY INFORMATION RECORD (Family Emergency & Peace of Mind Planner)
18. The Ultimate Therapist & Counselors Planner and Organizer
19. Building an Ethical Workplace
20. Managing Relationships at Work
21. Managing Business Meetings Effectively
22. Effective Delegation Skills
23. Goal Setting for Success
24. B2B Selling by Email
25. Professional Business Etiquette & Grooming
26. Dining Etiquette & Table Manners
27. Effective Networking Skills
28. Grooming, Etiquette & Manners for Teens, Young Adults & Future Leaders
29. Inter-Personal Skills
30. Get Ready, Get Hired!
31. Selling in a Recession
32. Effective Receivables Management in an Economic Downturn!
33. Real Estate & Property Sales Training

34. Credit Sales & Accounts Receivable Management
35. Selling Skills for Real Estate & Property Advisors
36. Take G.R.E.A.T. C.A.R.E!
37. Spa, Salon & Health Club Selling Skills
38. Selling Travel, Holiday & MICE Services
39. Selling Skills for Spa's, Salons & Health Clubs
40. Retailing in Salons & Spas
41. Selling Holiday, Vacation, Tours & Packages
42. The Power of Sales Referrals
43. Selling Luxury
44. Technical Selling Skills
45. Financial Advisors Sales Training
46. Dealing with Burnout at Work Monopolize Your Markets
47. Selling to Affluent Customers
48. Growing up with Grace
49. Financial Selling Skills
50. *The Effective Manager's Guide: Key Skills to Thrive*
51. From Aspiring to Inspiring: A Guide for New Managers on the Rise
52. The Power of Focus
53. Selling with Integrity: Sell Like Jesus The Perfect Role Model!
54. 31 Habits of Champions: Your 31-Day Journey to Greatness
55. Rejecting Grasshopper Talk: From Grasshopper to Giant-Killer-*Defeating Giants Daily!*
56. Navigate the AI-Powered Future of Bid & Proposals: Up-Skill to Stay Relevant with Alternative Career Paths & Opportunities
57. Hiring Sales Winners
58. Present with Impact
59. Success Unlocked: *Breaking Free from Habits that Hold You Back*
60. Complaints to Cheers, Feedback to Gold: Mastering Complaints Management
61. Thriving Together: *Cultivating Diversity, Equity, and Inclusion*
62. Coaching Skills for Sales Managers
63. Soaring to Success in Business & Leadership: Swifter, Higher, Stronger!
64. From Classroom to Podium: A Student's Guide to Powerful Public Speaking & Presentation Skills

65. Developing Self-Discipline
66. The CEO's 31-Day Power Plan: Unlocking Success through Essential Traits
67. Credibility Matters
68. A Winning Attitude
69. Bid & Proposal Management Using AI
70. Sales Forecasting: A Practical & Proven Guide to Strategic Sales Forecasting
71. Elevate & Energize: *50 Dynamic & Fun Activities for Peak Workplace Morale*
72. 'Sales SOS! Sales on Fire! *30 Days to Conquer Chaos & the Nightmares of Success!'*
73. Mastering Sales Managerial Skills: *Building High-Performing Teams & Driving Exceptional Results*
74. Eagle-Eyed Leadership: Unleashing the Power of 31 Lessons from Eagles
75. The Ultimate Employee Training Guide: *Training Today, Leading Tomorrow*
76. Being More Accountable at Work

Besides regularly contributing to business & trade journals, including international ones such as the 'Creative Training Techniques' and the 'Sales News' of the U.S.A, He is also a member of several prestigious bodies & trade associations, having participated in many Conferences & Workshops in India & Overseas.

Prior to his last assignment of leading & managing a large MNC as head, Gerard had a 3-year stint in the Middle East as a Consultant with a leading British Consultancy Firm.

As the past 'Official Country Representative' for the International Business Award- 'THE STEVIES'-(the business world's own Oscar) for about 4 years- he ensured a few Indian companies that qualify for the same every year!

Gerard can be contacted at:
Email: training@Sales-Training.in,training@CollectionSkills.com
Websites:
www.Sales-Training.in
www.EtiquetteWorks.in
www.CollectionSkills.com
www.RetailSalesTraining.in
www.SalesTrainingIndia.com
www.ManualPreparation.com
www.TrainingWithPuppets.com
www.FirstContactAcademy.com
www.SalesAndMarketingRecruiter.com

Our TRAININGS that can help your team

- ✓ **Sales Effectiveness**: Selling Skills for any Sector: Service/ Logistics/ FMCG Realty/ Insurance & Finance/ Media/ SPA's, Health Clubs & Salons/ Key Account Management, Effective Negotiation Skills/ Bid & Proposal Management Skills/ Retail Sales Training: Any Sector (Auto, Jewelry, Clothing, Luxury etc)
- ✓ **Customer Service Skills**-Complaints Handling & Customer Retention
- ✓ **Debt Prevention & Collection Skills**
- ✓ **Etiquette & Grooming**
- ✓ **Leadership & Managerial Skills**
- ✓ **Self & Personal Development Skills**: Presentation Skills/ Effective Communication Skills/Business Proposal Writing Skills/ Problem Solving & Decision Making Skills/ Empowering Secretaries-The perfect PA! (For Secretaries & PA's)/ Effective Time Management/ Teamwork & Teambuilding/ P.R.I.D.E- **P**ersonal **R**esponsibility **I**n **D**elivering **E**xcellence

www.ingramcontent.com/pod-product-compliance
Lightning Source LLC
LaVergne TN
LVHW010504160826
845677LV00012B/2649

* 9 7 8 9 3 9 2 4 9 2 4 9 5 *